D1523026

I GOT CAUGHT DRINKING AND DRIVING...
WHAT'S NEXT?

ELISSA BONGIORNO

ROSEN
PUBLISHING

NEW YORK

Published in 2022 by The Rosen Publishing Group, Inc.
29 East 21st Street, New York, NY 10010

Copyright © 2022 by The Rosen Publishing Group, Inc.

First Edition

Designer: Rachel Rising
Editor: Greg Roza

Portions of this work were originally authored by Valerie Mendralla and Janet
Grosshandler and published as *Drinking and Driving. Now What?* All new
material in this edition was authored by Elissa Bongiorno.

Library of Congress Cataloging-in-Publication Data

Names: Bongiorno, Elissa, author.
Title: I got caught drinking and driving ... what's next? / Elissa Bongiorno.
Description: NewYork :Rosen Publishing, [2022] | Series: Getting real |
Includes bibliographical references and index.
Identifiers: LCCN 2021003895 | ISBN 9781499470635 (library binding) | ISBN
9781499470628 (paperback) | ISBN 9781499470642 (ebook)
Subjects: LCSH: Drunk driving--United States--Juvenile literature. | Drunk
driving--Law and legislation--United States--Juvenile literature. |
Teenage automobile drivers--Alcohol use--United States--Juvenile
literature. | Teenagers--Alcohol use--United States--Juvenile
literature.
Classification: LCC HE5620.D72 B66 2022 | DDC 364.1/47--dc23
LC record available at https://lccn.loc.gov/2021003895

Some of the images in this book illustrate individuals who are
models. The depictions do not imply actual situations or events.

Manufactured in the United States of America

CPSIA Compliance Information: Batch #CSRYA22. For further information contact Rosen Publishing, New York, New York at 1-800-237-9932.

Find us on

CONTENTS

INTRODUCTION

Getting your driver's license can be an exciting time in your life. The ability to drive somewhere on your own can be exciting. Meeting your friends out for lunch, without your parents or other adults in the car, can be a lot of fun. Being able to drive to work or to head to the movies solo can provide an exciting taste of freedom. But it's important to remember that driving is a privilege, not a right. This means that when you're issued your driver's license, you must agree to follow the laws and regulations of the road. These laws are set by state governments around the country. One of the most important rules to remember is that you should never drink alcohol and then drive.

Getting your driver's license can be an exciting rite of passage in one's life. You can enjoy the freedom while still being careful and safe.

Drinking and driving kills one person about every 50 minutes. However, this is a simple situation for you to avoid. Just never, ever drink and drive.

That's because drinking and driving can be deadly. This is especially true for teens who are just learning how to handle vehicles on their own. Every day in the United States, about seven teens die in car crashes. It's the leading cause of death among adolescents. In nearly 25 percent of those crashes, the teen driver had been drinking alcohol. These deaths are preventable. Never drink and then drive.

Jessica Rasdall knows the dangers of drunk driving all too well. One night, Jessica got in a car accident while driving drunk. Jessica killed her best friend, who had been riding in the passenger seat. Her best friend since kindergarten was gone, and Jessica had to deal with the fact that she was responsible. She faced legal charges and her friend's angry family. Jessica's life changed in an instant.

Serious injuries can also be a consequence of drinking and driving. Sean Carter suffered a traumatic brain injury after getting in a truck with a friend who was driving drunk. He crashed the truck. Now Sean can no longer walk or talk out loud. He communicates by typing on a computer tablet. He now works with his mother to spread the word about the dangers of drunk driving so others don't make the same mistake he did.

Besides serious injury or death, driving drunk can have other serious outcomes. This is especially true when you're under the legal drinking age of 21. Suspended licenses, large fines, and even jail time can be part of the fallout from drinking and driving.

You could lose your job, your scholarship to college, and much more. It's just not worth the risk.

This book will help you understand what can happen when someone makes the decision to drink and drive and the real-life consequences of those actions. This way, you can better understand why your parents and teachers tell you to never drink alcohol and get behind the wheel of a car—or get into the car with a driver who's intoxicated. Through statistics, laws, and strategies, this book will help empower you to make responsible decisions when getting out on the road. If you or someone close to you has been arrested for drunk driving, this book will help you deal with the tconsequences. Driving can be a lot of fun and provide a lot of freedom, so long as you are safe and responsible while on the road.

The consequences of drunk driving can reach far beyond having to fix your car. There are fines, loss of license, and emotional fallout to deal with too.

CHAPTER 1

DRINKING AND DRIVING BY THE NUMBERS

We've all seen car accidents by the side of the road. It can be frightening to see smoking engines and twisted metal. Maybe the highway was slippery with ice, or a tire popped while someone was driving. Car accidents happen sometimes, but some accidents are preventable. Crashes caused by driving while texting, for example, have been particularly common since the rise in popularity of cell phones. The answer is simple: Never text and drive!

THE SCARY STATISTICS

There's never a good reason to drive while under the influence of alcohol. The cost of that decision can be incredibly high, but it can be prevented by making this simple choice. Tragically, thousands of Americans learn the same terrible lesson every year: Alcohol and driving do not mix. Here are some statistics:

• Some 2,121 drivers between the ages of 15 and 18 were killed in motor vehicle crashes in 2018.

• Of the 15- to 18-year-olds involved in fatal crashes in 2016, one in five of the drivers had been drinking.

• From 2005 to 2014, car-crash deaths among people ages 15 to 20 declined 51 percent and serious injuries were down 59 percent.

Drunk driving accidents can change people's lives forever, taking loved ones away and injuring others seriously. It's a problem that affects the whole community.

The decrease in motor vehicle crashes among teens does not mean that drinking and driving is not a serious problem. Thousands of teens are killed or seriously injured in alcohol-related crashes each year. Teens who get behind the wheel after drinking may also hurt innocent bystanders or other drivers.

PICTURES OF A CRASH-TEST DUMMY

In his book *Drinking and Driving: Know Your Limits and Liabilities*, Dr. Marshall B. Stearn discusses an eye-opening demonstration.

One Memorial Day weekend, the Madigan Army Hospital in Tacoma, Washington, documented the effects of a high-speed car crash. To promote a safety campaign, it sent a mannequin in a car moving at 55 miles (88.5 km) per hour crashing into a tree. With time-lapse photography, the following graphic sequence of events was captured:

• **ONE-TENTH OF A SECOND AFTER IMPACT:** The front bumper and chrome frosting of the grillwork collapse. Slivers of steel penetrate the tree to a depth of more than 1 inch (2.5 cm).

• **TWO-TENTHS OF A SECOND AFTER IMPACT:** The hood crumples and smashes into the windshield. Spinning rear wheels leave the ground. As the fender comes into contact with the tree, the car bends in the middle, with the rear end buckling over the front end.

• **THREE-TENTHS OF A SECOND AFTER IMPACT:** The mannequin's body is now off the seat, upright, knees pressing against the dashboard. The plastic and steel frame of the steering wheel begins to bend under the weight of the mannequin. Its head is near the sun visor, the chest above the steering column.

• **FOUR-TENTHS OF A SECOND AFTER IMPACT:** The car's front 24 inches (61 cm) have been demolished, but the rear end is still traveling at an estimated 35 miles (56 km) per hour. The mannequin is still traveling at 55 miles (88.5 km) per hour. The heavy engine block crunches into the tree. The rear end of the car, still bucking like a horse, rises high enough to scrape bark off low branches.

• **FIVE-TENTHS OF A SECOND AFTER IMPACT:** The mannequin's hands, frozen onto the steering wheel, bend the steering column into an almost vertical position. The force of gravity then pushes its body into the steering column.

• **SIX-TENTHS OF A SECOND AFTER IMPACT:** The brake pedal shears off at the floorboard. The chassis bends in the middle, shearing body bolts. The rear of the car begins to fall back down; its spinning wheels dig into the ground.

• **SEVEN-TENTHS OF A SECOND AFTER IMPACT:** The seat of the car rams forward, pinning the mannequin against the steering shaft; the hinges tear, and the doors spring open.

Close your eyes and see yourself as the driver or passenger of this car. It doesn't take much imagination to conjure up the ghastly picture of what happens to the people inside. Even if you were the best driver in the world, it would be almost impossible to respond quickly enough to such an emergency: seven-tenths of a second pass and it's over. Even if an air bag inflated, imagine the force of the impact if the car were traveling even faster. Add to this scenario the effect of alcohol on the driver. Making immediate and appropri-

(continued on the next page)

(continued from the previous page)

ate judgments in trying to avoid this tragic event would not be possible.

"I'm OK to drive" is the oft-repeated statement when a party is breaking up. Believing that your driving skills are as good when you're drinking as they are when you're sober is a common effect of alcohol. In several studies, drivers knocked over orange cones and ran down flags in a driving course, but they still believed they drove as well as they did when not drunk. To drive safely and minimize the risks of getting in a motor vehicle crash, you need to be sharp, alert, and in control. Drinking interferes with your emotions, your brain, your coordination, and all of the skills necessary to drive safely.

EXPERIENCE MATTERS

No matter how old you are or how much driving experience you have, drinking and driving is always dangerous. However, your chances of being in a motor vehicle crash increase when you get into a car with another teen driver. Teens have less driv-

Teens may feel very confident about their driving when they first get their license. But statistics show that the more experience you have behind the wheel, the safer you will drive.

ing experience than adults. As a result, they have a greater risk of being in a collision, even without the influence of alcohol. New drivers are more likely to get in an accident in the first few months of receiving their license. Per mile driven, a 16-year-old is nearly 1.5 times as likely to get in a crash as an 18- or 19-year-old driver. This is because driving is a skill, and you get better at it over time.

MORE LIKELY

Although drinking and driving occurs among teens of both sexes, statistics indicate that boys are more likely to be involved in fatal crashes, especially when alcohol is a factor. The Centers for Disease Control (CDC) reports that in 2017, crashes among drivers between 16 and 20 years of age were more likely to have involved alcohol if the driver was male. Twenty percent of male drivers ages 15 to 20 involved in fatal crashes were drinking at the time, as compared to 15 percent of female drivers in the same age group.

SEAT BELTS SAVE LIVES

The use of seat belts is also a factor in the outcome of alcohol-related car crashes. Wearing a seat belt can increase your chances of surviving a crash. When drinking, teens are less likely to wear seat belts. That's because alcohol can impair your ability to make good decisions. According to the CDC, 58 percent of young drivers who were involved in fatal alcohol-related crashes in 2017 were not wearing seat belts. The drunk driver is often not the victim in the accident that they've caused. Many times, it's the passenger who's killed because they didn't wear a seat belt.

Always wear your seat belt when driving or riding in a car. It could save your life!

MYTHS AND FACTS ABOUT DRINKING AND DRIVING

- **MYTH #1**: All teens drink alcohol.

- **FACT #1**: If you feel like you're the only teen not drinking alcohol, you're wrong. Only about 29 percent of high school students reported drinking during the last 30 days, according to the 2019 Youth Risk Behavior Survey from the CDC.

- **MYTH #2**: There are things you can do to reduce your level of inebriation, such as taking a shower, drinking coffee, or drinking water.

- **FACT #2**: Time is the only thing that can reduce your level of inebriation. Once alcohol enters the bloodstream, it takes the body about one hour to eliminate the alcohol in one drink. The human body eliminates alcohol at the average rate of 0.016 blood alcohol concentration (BAC) per hour. There's nothing you can do to speed up this process.

- **MYTH #3**: If you're just driving a short distance, it won't matter if you have one drink.

- **FACT #3**: Eighty-eight percent of motor vehicle accidents happen within 10 miles of home. This means that even if you're driving near your home or your friend's house, it's always important to be a responsible driver.

CHAPTER 2

YOUR BODY ON ALCOHOL

You're at a party, having fun with your friends. Loud music is playing. Someone you like is nearby, smiling at you. Someone else passes you a cup full of beer. You think, "What harm could it do? I'll only have one." But even one drink can affect your motor skills, your decision making, and your ability to drive.

Driving requires many skills, sharp senses, lots of concentration, and quick reaction time. Drivers who have been drinking alcohol are not effective at putting it all together. Even a small amount of alcohol can impair your driving ability. In 2018, the NHTSA reported that 1,878 people were killed in crashes involving alcohol where the driver had a low amount of alcohol in their bloodstream. Here's what happens to your body when you drink alcohol.

ALCOHOL'S PATHWAY

Alcohol affects the central nervous system and the brain, which in turn affect the entire body. When you drink alcohol, it can enter the bloodstream directly

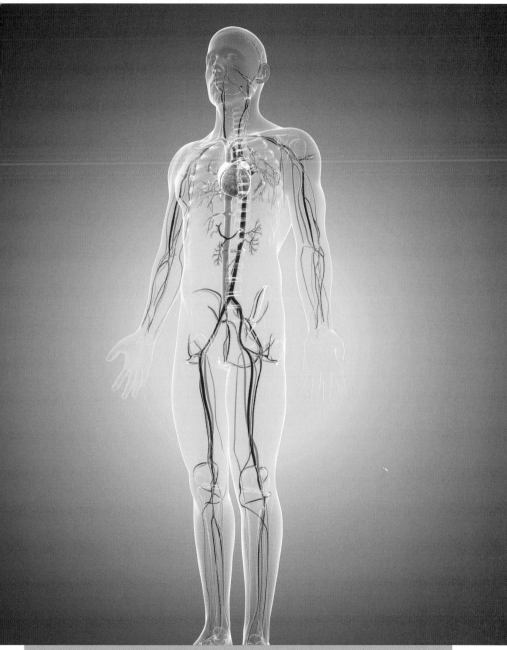

Alcohol affects the central nervous system after being absorbed into your body. This means it can alter all of the body's processes, including breathing and movement.

without being digested. Researchers say that small amounts are absorbed directly through the lining of the mouth and throat. Most of the alcohol goes through the walls of the stomach and small intestine and is absorbed into the blood. Once alcohol is absorbed into the bloodstream, it works to slow the functioning of the central nervous system. The central nervous system includes the brain and spinal cord, and it controls almost all of the body's functions. From there, alcohol travels to the brain and other organs of the body. How intoxicated a person gets depends on their age, weight, sex, how fast they drink, and how much food is in their stomach.

Most of the alcohol that a person drinks is processed in the liver. Enzymes in the liver break down the alcohol, and it eventually leaves the body in the breath, sweat, and urine. The body breaks down alcohol slowly. If a person drinks more than he or she can eliminate in a certain time, the drug accumulates in the body. The person becomes intoxicated, which means that the poisonous or toxic effects of alcohol go into action in the brain and the body. As a result, the person feels drunk.

BLOOD ALCOHOL CONCENTRATION

Blood alcohol concentration (BAC) refers to the amount of alcohol in a person's blood. The more alcohol that is taken in, the more the percentage of alcohol in the blood rises. Drivers with high blood alcohol content are at a greatly increased risk for crashes, injuries, and deaths on the road.

BAC is always written as a decimal part of 1 percent. For example, if a person has a BAC of 0.1 percent, it means the person has one part alcohol to a thousand parts of blood in their body. BAC can be measured using a breath, blood, or urine test. As a person's BAC rises, the effects of alcohol become more pronounced. To show what happens to people when blood alcohol content rises, researchers have described five levels of intoxication:

LEVEL 1: A person has a moderate amount to drink (about one drink for women or two drinks for men) in a period of one to two hours. The person's blood alcohol concentration is in the range of 0.01 to 0.05 percent. At this stage, the alcohol may make a person feel happy, relaxed, talkative, flirty, and confident. However, if the person has a BAC of more than 0.03 percent, his or her driving skills are already affected.

LEVEL 2: Continuing to drink will boost the blood alcohol concentration to between 0.05 and 0.08 percent. Alcohol reaches further into the higher learning center of the brain. While the person may feel and act self-confident, their reaction time, judgment, senses, and movement are impaired.

LEVEL 3: When the blood alcohol concentration reaches 0.08 to 0.15 percent, the person is in a risky state. Thoughts can become muddled, and speech can become slurred. Vision and hearing are affected as well. Balance, coordination, and muscle control are impaired, sometimes resulting in staggering. The individual may have nausea or vomiting. At or above 0.08 BAC, a person is considered legally intoxicated.

LEVEL 4: From 0.15 to 0.30 BAC, the person is in a high-risk state. All physical and mental functions are impaired considerably. The person is unable to walk without help. Breathing is labored, body temperature may go down, and reflexes are depressed. There may be a loss of bladder control. The person does not know what he or she is doing or saying and is unable to remember events. Loss of consciousness may occur.

LEVEL 5: Above a 0.30 BAC, a person is unconscious or in a coma. The part of the brain that controls breathing and heartbeat is dangerously affected. The person is close to death and could die without medical attention.

The more alcohol one takes into their body, the more drunk feelings can intensify and grow out of control. Eventually, large alcohol intake can lead to unconsciousness.

ESTIMATING YOUR BAC

You can figure out your blood alcohol concentration level while drinking, thanks to a formula developed by researchers. To begin, know that "one drink" includes all of the following:

- 12 ounces (355 ml) of beer
- 5 ounces (148 ml) of wine
- 1.5 ounces (44 ml) of hard liquor

These are standard servings of alcohol, but be aware that alcoholic drinks can vary in terms of content and strength. To calculate BAC, you need to know your weight, how many drinks you've had, and how long you've been drinking. You also need a chart showing average BACs.

For example, imagine that a 180-pound (81.6 kg) man had four drinks two hours ago. Looking at the chart, you can see that his BAC would have been 0.08 then. To find out how long the alcohol will be in his body, use this calculation: Alcohol leaves the body on an average of 0.015 per hour (for men) and 0.018 per hour (for women). So, if the man had those four drinks two hours ago: 0.015 x 2 = 0.03. And 0.08 – 0.03 is 0.05. The man's BAC would be about 0.05 now.

By looking at a BAC chart and thinking about these numbers, you can quickly see that even a small amount of alcohol makes it too dangerous to drive, especially for those under the age of 21.

Be aware that different types of alcoholic drinks contain different percentages of alcohol. This means some drinks will get one drunker than others, and more quickly.

ALCOHOL AND EYESIGHT

Drinking alcohol affects a person's vision. Since alcohol is a depressant, it relaxes all the muscles in the body. A person under the influence of alcohol has less control over their muscles, including those that move and focus the eyes.

When an eye is working properly, light enters through the pupil and goes through the lens. The lens focuses light rays on the retina. If something interferes with this process, the impulses, or messages, that are sent to the brain are distorted. If a fuzzy picture is sent to the brain, the mind cannot correctly interpret the traffic scene in view.

Alcohol also affects eye focus. A muscle in the eye automatically brings into focus objects both near and far. With the relaxing effect of alcohol, that muscle cannot function properly. Therefore, the person does not see clearly. What they see is blurry.

In addition, alcohol affects how the eyes react to light. The pupil of the eye acts like the shutter of a camera to let in just the right amount of light. The pupil narrows when bright light enters the eye in order to prevent damage to the retina. In the dark, the pupil opens to admit more light, making it easier for a person to see. When a person is driving at night and the headlights of oncoming cars shine into their eyes, it takes one second for the pupils to contract and seven seconds for them to adapt again to the dark. When a person is drinking, the process doesn't happen as quickly. The pupils contract, but it takes them longer to recover. As a result, one can

BLOOD ALCOHOL CONCENTRATION (BAC)
NUMBER OF DRINKS AND BAC IN 2 HOURS OF DRINKING

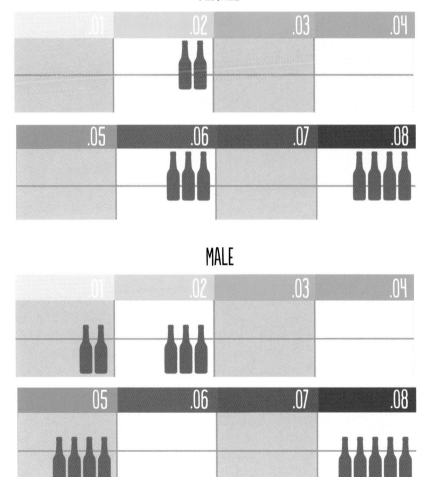

FEMALE

MALE

By looking at this BAC chart, someone can get an idea how much alcohol is in their system. Even one or two drinks can have an effect on behavior or reflexes, even if you don't realize it.

Alcohol has a relaxing effect on the whole body, including the eyes. This means it can be hard to read street signs if driving while drunk.

be driving semi-blind for several seconds. Remember the crash test dummy? The car was flattened within a second. There's no extra time to react when you're driving.

Drinking alcohol can also lead to double vision. Six muscles act to make the eyes work together. When these muscles are impaired by alcohol, it's difficult for the eyes to focus on the same point. Double vision can result. It may look like two cars are approaching instead of one. Which of the two cars do you avoid?

In addition, the eyes need to work together to judge distances. Changing lanes, passing other cars, and many other driving skills depend on how well a person can judge distances. When a person is drunk, no clearly coordinated picture is sent to the brain. Depth perception is altered. One has difficulty deciding exactly how far away that other car is.

Finally, alcohol affects one's peripheral vision, or the ability to see things outside the central area of focus. Being able to see cars coming out of intersections or driveways and reacting when people walk into the road are crucial abilities when driving. If you notice fewer dangers on either side of you as you drive, you increase your chances of having a motor vehicle crash. Speed also affects peripheral vision. The faster you drive, the less peripheral vision you have. Add the effects of alcohol, and you get a driver who sees almost nothing besides the blurry, distorted scene right in front of him or her.

PAYING ATTENTION WHILE DRUNK

Driving requires a person to monitor many things at once. Their attention is divided among the many tasks and skills needed to drive safely. A new driver is inexperienced at mentally processing all the information gathered as they drive. And remember, studies show new drivers are more likely to crash even if they haven't been drinking. In addition to all the other things a driver needs to accomplish, add the effects of a loud radio, a cell phone, or distractions from passengers. The brain must analyze all of this incoming data. The driver makes and executes decisions based on the brain's conclusions. Alcohol makes it much harder for the driver to manage multiple streams of information effectively and react appropriately. A driver who has been drinking will find it difficult to sort out distractions and focus on the most important thing: driving.

Continual observation of everything in the field of vision—other cars moving in one's direction, stoplights, traffic signs, parked cars, pedestrians, motorcycles, bicycles, and road conditions—is vital to safety. A driver must always be alert. Careful observation can be the difference between a safe ride home and a crash. A person uses visual search and recognition skills to sort out all that they encounter while driving.

Just looking through the windshield isn't enough to take in all that requires attention. Using the rearview mirror and the side mirrors, turning one's head to see out the side windows and the back, and checking the car's blind spots are all part of searching out and recognizing potential problems.

In laboratory tests and in a report by the U.S. Department of Transportation, it has been documented that drinking impairs people's ability to divide attention among the tasks necessary to drive safely. Alcohol also slows the rate at which the brain processes information, interfering with its ability to register important messages.

DELAYED REACTION TIME

Reaction time, or the time it takes to begin responding to a situation, is crucial in driving. Slamming on your brakes, veering to the side of the road, or scooting into the other lane to avoid a collision

It's never safe to drink and drive. Even if you think you feel fine, if you've been drinking, your abilities and senses are impaired. Driving requires all these abilities and senses.

requires a quick reaction in addition to the previously mentioned driving skills. Alcohol consumption is known to slow a person's reaction time, and the effect worsens the more one drinks.

The effects of alcohol on your body are serious. Your vision, reaction time, and attention span are all negatively impacted by drinking. And that can seriously affect your ability to drive safely.

CHAPTER 3

BUT YOUR FRIENDS ARE DOING IT

It may seem like alcohol is everywhere around you. Television commercials and advertisements often give the idea of how cool and fun it can be to drink. In movies and on TV shows, teens are shown drinking beer at parties. Maybe your parents let you have a glass of wine with dinner sometimes. Perhaps they let you have a glass of champagne on holidays or to celebrate special occasions. You may have friends who are starting to experiment with alcohol too. It can be confusing to figure out when it's OK to drink alcohol and when it's not. Just remember that actions have consequences, and alcohol can affect your ability to make decisions. And it's never a smart idea to drink and drive.

IS EVERYONE DRINKING?

"Monitoring the Future" is a yearly survey of alcohol and drug use among more than 42,000 eighth, tenth, and twelfth graders all over the country. It has been conducted every year since 1975 by the Institute for Social Research at the University of Michigan, Ann Arbor, and is funded by the National Institute on Drug Abuse.

Students in the survey reveal information about their use of drugs and alcohol. According to the 2019 survey results, there has been a significant decrease in the percentage of all age ranges surveyed who said they drank alcohol. In fact, it was more than a 20 percent decrease for all age ranges, which is great news. Alcohol, however, remains one of the top drugs used among teens.

Even though teen drinking may be decreasing, the numbers from the survey still show that many high school students do drink alcohol. More than

You need to be at least 21 in all U.S. states to buy alcohol. Breaking this law can get you in big trouble, and there may also be consequences with your school or job.

50 percent of high school seniors surveyed said they had drunk alcohol in the past year. Nearly 20 percent of eighth graders said the same. Binge drinking is also a problem. Although it's also on the decline, more than 14 percent of high school seniors reported drinking more than five alcoholic beverages in a row in the past two weeks.

Peer pressure can make you feel like you have to drink alcohol to be able to hang out with your friends. It's normal to want to fit in. But you have to make the right decision for you, not anyone else.

THE POWER OF PEER PRESSURE

Having fun. Letting loose. Getting up the courage to talk to someone you like. There are lots of reasons why teens drink, and peer pressure is one of them. A teen can head to a party planning on having fun with friends while sober, only to end up drunk because friends were egging them on. When it's time to leave a party, finding a sober driver can be tough. It's hard for someone to admit that they've had too much and shouldn't drive. Drinking impairs a person's judgment; you may not even realize that you're too drunk to drive. An intoxicated person might become angry if others suggest that they shouldn't drive. More often than not, teens will get behind the wheel—or into someone else's car—when they shouldn't.

Being a teen can be stressful. With parents, school, social media, and more pressures, there are many reasons alcohol may seem like a good way to relax. You may feel tense or anxious and want to feel better. You can be bored, bitter, or angry and think alcohol is the answer. You may just want to have fun.

But as much as your friends may try to convince you to have a drink of alcohol, you can also influence them to do something else instead. A study done by neuroscientists at Virginia Polytechnic Institute found that when teens observe their friends making a safe decision—like choosing not to drink alcohol—those friends were more likely to make a safe choice too. That's something to think about the next time someone hands you an alcoholic beverage.

ADOLESCENTS AND ALCOHOLISM

Drinking alcohol can have a lot of serious consequences for your health. Research shows that if a person begins drinking at an early age, he or she is more likely to be a heavy drinker in the teen years and as an adult. According to the National Survey on Drug Use and Health, almost 500,000 teens in the United States have alcohol use disorder. This means that they can have problems controlling their drinking, having to drink more and more alcohol to achieve the same drunk feeling, and more. It can cause distress and make it hard to function in regular day-to-day life.

Alcohol can also harm teen brain development—your brain is not done growing until you're in your early 20s. The prefrontal cortex portion of the brain, responsible for controlling impulses, is the last part of your brain to fully develop. And it can be affected by alcohol abuse.

How your parents drink also influences your drinking habits. In fact, most kids have their first drink at home. Unfortunately, alcohol use disorder develops more quickly and with less alcohol for teens than for adults. A young person can become an alcoholic in one or two years.

You may have heard of something called tolerance. Tolerance means that with frequent drinking over time, the brain can change its sensitivity to alcohol and "tolerate" higher levels. As a result, the person needs to drink more alcohol to feel any of its effects. Developing tolerance can be a symptom of alcohol dependence.

Drinking alcohol frequently as a teen can have serious consequences. Alcohol can harm brain development. Teens can also be at a greater risk for addiction.

SOCIAL MEDIA STRESSORS

Social media can be a stressful landscape for teens to navigate, and it can make you feel like everyone is having a much better time than you are. Social media can influence your behavior, whether you know it's happening or not. In a study done at Michigan State University, social media users who saw a beer ad were more likely to drink a beer afterward, as opposed to those who saw an ad for water. It's important to be aware that what's happening on social media is only someone's perception of reality, not real life.

Still not convinced? Think about what you post on social media every day. Do you say that you're bored and haven't done anything interesting all weekend? Or do you post the pic of the one fun thing you did all day and make it look like you're having the best time ever? Lots of other people are doing the same thing!

PLAN WHILE YOU CAN

Another way to avoid an uncomfortable situation where you need to say no to a friend is to "Plan While You Can." The campaign, from the state of Texas, suggests four ideas to help. Consider these ideas before going to an event where people might be drinking alcohol.

A recent study found that seeing alcohol on social media can make you more likely to drink. What you see online can influence your actions, whether you realize it or not.

Designate a sober driver. Before you leave to go anywhere, talk with your friends and decide who will drive. This person must stay sober all night, no matter what.

Call a cab or use a ride share. Ride-sharing apps can be a big help in avoiding drinking and driving. If you're in a place without a sober driver to take you home, consider calling a cab or using an app to get a driver to take you home. On most ride-sharing apps, you need to be 18 to be a passenger, but it can be a good option to keep in mind.

HOW TO SAY NO

It can be hard to say no to a friend who's offering you an alcoholic drink or a ride home—or asking for a ride home. It can be even harder to say no if you've been drinking too. Your judgement can be impaired. This is why it can be a good idea to practice saying no ahead of time.

The ideas below are taken from a youth character-building program started by Leah Davies of Bend, Oregon. She has trained many parents, school counselors, and teachers through her Kelly Bear Character and Resiliency Education Skills Program. The program suggests eight different ways to say no when someone is encouraging you to do something risky:

- **SAY "NO" OR "NO, THANKS," OVER AND OVER IF NECESSARY.**
Tell the person, "No, thanks. I don't drink," or "No, I'm the designated driver tonight."

• CALL IT WHAT IT IS.

"That's using drugs, and I don't do that."

"That's against the law for us, and I don't want to get in trouble."

• TALK ABOUT SOMETHING ELSE.

Change the subject: "That was a great game!"

"Have you finished that project yet?"

• ASK QUESTIONS.

Turn it back to the friend: "Why do you care if I drink or not?"

"Why would you want me to drink and drive?"

• GIVE REASONS.

"I don't want to risk losing my license or getting into a crash."

"My parents would never trust me with the car again."

• USE HUMOR OR SARCASM.

"Are you kidding? Beer can really mess up my buff body."

"Sure, that's all I need to do. I'd be grounded for the rest of my life!"

• SUGGEST DOING SOMETHING ELSE.

"Let's call my mom. She'll pick us up no matter what time it is."

"How about leaving this party now?"

"Let's do something else that doesn't involve drinking."

• IF YOU WANT THEIR FRIENDSHIP, KEEP THE DOOR OPEN.

"If you decide to do something that doesn't involve alcohol, let me know."

These refusal skills will give you a handle on turning peer pressure to your advantage. They will help keep you safe and alive.

Friends
don't let friends
drive drunk.

If your friend has had too much to drink, he doesn't have to drive.
Here are three ways to keep your friend alive …

drive your friend home

have your friend sleep over

U.S.Department of Transportation
National Highway Traffic Safety
Administration

call a cab

Having a plan before you go out is always a great idea. It can help prepare you for what to do if you or your driver end up drinking. Plan ahead and stay alive.

Use mass transit. If you live somewhere with buses and trains, mass transit can be another great choice to get home safely. Check the schedule before you leave.

Spend the night. If none of these other options are available to you, consider a sleepover. Remember that the only thing that can get alcohol out of your system is time. The morning after a party with alcohol can be a much safer time to drive.

It can be hard to say no to a friend, but you now have some ideas about how deal with the peer pressure surrounding alcohol and drinking and driving. True friends will understand that you're making the choice to keep yourself and others safe from the deadly consequences of drunk driving.

CHAPTER 4

THE RULES OF THE ROAD

Drinking and driving is incredibly dangerous—not to mention stupid. You could kill yourself or someone else, a passenger in your car or a stranger you've never met. There are other serious consequences to drinking and driving because it's against the law. If caught, you could be arrested and charged.

IT'S THE LAW

Laws about drinking and driving have gotten stricter, especially for teens. It's illegal in every state for people under the age of 21 to buy, possess, or drink alcohol or transport open alcoholic beverages. It's also illegal for someone under 21 to drink at all and then drive. These laws penalize young people for operating a vehicle with any trace of alcohol in their systems. Depending on the state, even a negligible level, such as 0.01 or 0.02 BAC, may get you in trouble.

If a police officer suspects someone is driving while drunk, they can pull them over. They will give them tests to check their sobriety.

If police officers have probable cause to believe that a driver has been drinking, zero-tolerance laws allow them to give breath tests to those under 21. If a driver refuses the test, or if the test shows any level of alcohol in the blood, the driver can face the following consequences:

- Fines up to $1,000
- Mandatory loss of driving privileges for six months to a year
- Community service
- Participation in an alcohol education and highway safety program
- Additional penalties as imposed by a judge

If a person is not driving but is caught drinking while underage, some of the same penalties might apply. One can temporarily lose driving privileges, even if no car is involved. For those who do not yet have a driver's license, the suspension starts when they are eligible.

More license suspension time can be added if a person is drinking while in a motor vehicle, even if he or she is not the driver. If caught, a person can be required to successfully complete an alcohol rehabilitation program.

The CDC reports that drivers ages 16 to 20 are 17 times more likely to die in a car crash when their BAC is 0.08 or higher. Strict enforcement of zero-tolerance laws can prevent many fatal crashes every year. These zero-tolerance laws support existing state laws that forbid the sale and serving of alcohol to underage drinkers. Keeping teens alive is the main reason for these new, stricter laws.

PARTY FOUL

Some teens may ask, "What about drinking at your own or someone else's house? My parents say they would rather know where and with whom I'm drinking, so they let us stay at my house and drink."

Usually, social host liability laws make this kind of activity illegal. Charges can be filed against property owners, parents, or guardians that allow underage use of alcohol or drugs on the premises. If minors are drinking on private property and the owner, parents, or guardians are present, they can be arrested and charged with allowing underage drinking, as well as creating and maintaining a condition that endangers the safety and health of individuals.

Even if the drinking occurs when the owners, parents, or guardians are not present, they can still be held liable. Sometimes, teens plan a party when someone's parents aren't home. The police may break up the party, but by then damage may have occurred to the house, property, or people. The parents may have to spend money to repair the damages or compensate other parents for what happened to their kids at the party. They may also face civil or criminal fines, imprisonment, and the threat of being sued for emotional pain and suffering.

GETTING A DRIVER'S LICENSE

Teens now must adhere to graduated driver licensing laws, meant to help keep new drivers safe. Although all states have their own laws regarding learner's permits and driver's licenses, there are typically three stages to getting a full license.

STAGE ONE: LEARNER'S PERMIT A teen can get a learner's permit between the ages of 14 and 16, depending on the state. This means you can drive when in the car with a licensed driver over 21 years of age. You must practice for many hours, get in no crashes, and keep entertainment (such as music) off.

STAGE TWO: INTERMEDIATE (PROVISIONAL) LICENSE The number of passengers a driver can have in the car is limited during stage two. Night driving hours are also restricted, and the driver must have a licensed driver in the car. Entertainment stays off too. This stage can last up to one year.

STAGE THREE: FULL LICENSE Once the other two stages are completed and the driver turns 18 years old, passenger and night restrictions are lifted. Alcohol is still not allowed.

Imagine this scenario: you have a party at a friend's house, and it gets a little wild toward the end. Two guys get into a fight, and one of them gets his front teeth knocked out. There are broken beer bottles and blood all over the rug and furniture in the living room. The parents of the injured person threaten to sue your friend's parents, who didn't even know about the party, for negligence.

If alcohol is served in a home, the adults (anyone over 21) may be held liable for any person who is injured as a result of underage drinking in their home, in their vehicles, or on their property. Involvement in such an activity could lead to the loss of a home or other assets, jail time, and fines.

Driving with an instructor before you get your license or permit can help you learn how to operate a car safely. By practicing, you can become a safe driver who can enjoy the open road!

Serving alcohol at your home can get your parents in big trouble with the law. Social host liability laws can have far-reaching consequences if someone gets hurt at your party.

Stiffer penalties for underage drinking aim to keep teens alcohol-free. A person who hasn't had any alcohol is less likely to be a danger to others on the road.

Several states have enacted laws for accomplices to underage drinking. People who are 21 or older who purchase alcohol or provide alcohol to underage individuals may be subject to:

- Fines of up to $2,000
- A misdemeanor charge of contributing to the delinquency of a minor
- Retail license suspension
- Possible jail time/probation

Adults who let a minor use their identification for the purpose of buying alcoholic beverages can face the above consequences, plus:

- Fines up to $1,000
- Arrest
- Up to six months of imprisonment

States continue to move in the direction of tougher penalties for underage drinkers. States hope the stronger laws will deter young people from drinking and driving. They're also designed to provide early detection and treatment for those who show a tendency toward alcohol abuse.

0.08 BAC IS TOO MUCH

By 2005, the federal government required each state to pass a 0.08 BAC "per se" law or lose federal funding. These laws mean that for those over 21, it's illegal to drive with an alcohol concentration at or above 0.08. It doesn't matter if the person shows other signs of intoxication (slurred speech, erratic driving, or loss of balance, for example) or not.

These laws were passed because research indicates that even at low blood alcohol levels, many drivers are impaired and present a danger to themselves and to others. Tolerance varies from person to person. Some drivers have problems driving even with a 0.02 BAC level. At 0.08, even experienced drivers are affected. Studies by NHTSA and other agencies show that 0.08 BAC laws reduce alcohol-related crashes and fatalities by 10.4 percent. This means that 0.08 BAC per se laws have saved 1,736 lives annually and a total of 24,868 lives between 1983 and 2014!

The 0.08 BAC per se laws have been so successful that some are considering lowering the BAC limit to 0.05. Other countries have successfully implemented this ruling. Estimates say a 0.05 BAC law could save 1,790 lives annually. Utah was the first state to pass a 0.05 BAC limit in 2018.

A breathalyzer test can be administered by a police officer when they pull you over. If your BAC comes back over a certain level, they can take your license away immediately.

IMMEDIATE LICENSE REMOVAL

Another way lawmakers are trying to stop people from drinking and driving is with administrative license revocation, or ALR. ALR allows an arresting officer to immediately take away the license of any driver who is found with a BAC at or above the legal limit. They can also take the license of anyone who refuses to take a BAC test.

Here's how it works: Drivers pulled over on suspicion of drinking and driving are asked to take a field sobriety test (e.g., walking a straight line, saying the alphabet) and/or breath test to assess the alcohol concentration in their body. If a person fails the test or refuses to take it, their driver's license can be automatically revoked, even before going to court.

The person may get a temporary driving permit for a short time, such as two or three weeks, and then the driver is notified of their right to appeal the revocation. If there's no appeal, or if the revocation is upheld, the offender loses the right to drive for a set period of time (90 days for a first offense in most states and longer for subsequent offenses).

As of 2017, 41 states have ALR laws. A study from the academic journal *Traffic Injury Prevention* showed that states with ALR laws have lower rates of drinking and driving than states without the restriction. The study also found that states with longer license suspension periods (91 to 180 days or even 180-plus days) had even lower rates of drinking and driving.

ALR laws are effective because they immediately punish a drunk driver for breaking the law. They are also a deterrent. Drivers who are arrested and have their licenses revoked under ALR laws are less likely to drink and drive again. People who have not been arrested are also discouraged from drinking and driving because they know they can lose their license immediately if they're caught.

NOW WHAT?

Unfortunately, despite efforts to prevent people from drinking and driving, many make the mistake of doing it anyway. The consequences of this mistake are serious. The following are typical repercussions of driving under the influence of alcohol.

YOU'RE UNDER ARREST

Getting caught drinking and driving can lead to your arrest. This is a serious and expensive situation. Lawyer's fees, fines, and time in jail can be the results of being convicted of DUI (driving under the influence).

A person who is arrested for drunk driving must appear in court. The judge decides the sentence. A DUI conviction makes a person a criminal. A person who is convicted has to face the consequences, which can include the following legal penalties, according to the Insurance Institute for Highway Safety and the Governors Highway Safety Association.

• **Fines.** Each state has specific laws. For DUI, offenders can expect to pay various fines for a first conviction.

• **Jail.** Spending anywhere from 48 hours to a year in jail can be a penalty for a first-time DUI. Some states allow offenders to do community service instead of jail time by working in their town or community rebuilding, cleaning up, or helping others.

• **Probation.** Instead of jail time, a few states may place offenders on probation. This means that the person's behavior and lifestyle are monitored for a period of time, possibly one to three years. The probation officer may check with the person's family, school, and employer to make sure he or she is staying out of trouble. The offender must report to the probation officer once a month or at appointed times.

• **Rehabilitation.** Some DUI laws require offenders to complete a driver improvement program. Many states also require offenders to undergo an alcohol rehabilitation program to help them recognize and deal with their drinking problem.

• **License revocation.** A person convicted of DUI will lose his or her license for at least several months, perhaps as long as a year.

• **Ignition interlock.** All 50 states now use ignition interlocks for convicted DUI offenders, sometimes even for the first offense. An ignition interlock is a system where the offender blows into a device installed in their car that can detect their BAC. The car cannot be started if the person's BAC is above a certain level (usually 0.02 to 0.04).

FINANCIAL AND PERSONAL PROBLEMS

Being arrested for drunk driving can cause financial and personal difficulties. For example, you might need to hire a lawyer to help you fight a DUI arrest. Add to that expense the fine you'll have to pay if you're convicted.

In addition, your auto insurance premium will inevitably rise. Insurance companies do not like risky drivers because chances are high that such drivers will cost them a lot of money. Since you must insure your vehicle by law, an alcohol-related conviction can cost you for many years to come.

A DUI conviction can lead to job loss. Employers cannot rely on you if you're not able to get to work, whether it's a part-time job after school or full-time employment. License revocation can mean a quick end to your job, especially one in which you are required to drive.

If you're arrested and convicted of DUI, it's not pleasant for your family either. The worry, stress, and anxiety that you, your parents, and other family members will experience in this situation may be overwhelming. Arguments, accusations, and denials are possible outcomes. Many newspapers report the names of those convicted of DUI.

The consequences of DUI outlined above are for first-time offenders. According to the National Highway Traffic Safety Administration, the average total cost for a first-time offender could be $10,000! Things get more serious if you are convicted a second time within a certain number of years. A third

Being convicted of DUI can change your life forever. And if you've hurt or killed someone while driving, the consequences will be even stronger.

conviction increases jail time and fines.

It's a different story if you're convicted of DUI and have caused injury or death to another person. People convicted in these circumstances can spend years in prison, pay heavy fines, and lose their licenses for quite a few years. There are also serious emotional consequences, including feelings of guilt for having hurt or killed another person.

The laws in each state may vary. Laws may also change often. Check with your local police department or state department of motor vehicles for your state's laws.

Drinking and driving can have serious consequences for you and your family. Be sure to remember that when you're around alcohol.

10 GREAT QUESTIONS TO ASK A POLICE OFFICER ABOUT DRUNK DRIVING

1. What are the drinking and driving statistics for my state?
2. Are there social host liability laws here?
3. Where can I go if I need help with my drinking?
4. What should I do if someone I know is going to drink and drive?
5. How can I resist peer pressure?
6. What other issues should teens in our community look out for?
7. Are there laws against biking or boating while drunk?
8. What effects of drinking and driving have you seen at work?
9. Do we have sobriety checkpoints here?
10. What would you say to someone who is about to drink and drive?

A police officer may be able to offer you good advice about avoiding drinking and driving. Many officers have likely had to respond to drunk-driving crashes, and they know better than most the heartbreak and trouble these actions can cause.

CHAPTER 5

WHAT HAPPENS AFTER: CONSEQUENCES OF DRINKING AND DRIVING

So, you made the bad decision to drink and drive. You got caught, or you were in an accident. Maybe your friend got hurt. Maybe a stranger died. What happens now?

REAL LIVES, REAL STORIES

Sometimes, those who've dealt with the consequences of drinking and driving choose to share their stories. They hope that this way others won't make the same mistake. RADD, an organization of the entertainment industry, and coalition members including HBO Family, the National Organizations for Youth Safety (NOYS), and NHTSA created a documentary called *Smashed*. The film is meant to show the real, long-term effects of injury caused by underage drinking and driving. This TV-14 rated, graphic presentation takes place at the University

Being in a car accident can be a terrifying and violent experience. Drinking and driving can cause injuries to yourself and others and even death.

of Maryland Shock Trauma Center in Baltimore and chronicles the stories of real teen crash victims who did not die. Below are synopses of some of the true stories featured in *Smashed*:

• **Timmy, age 15:** After drinking a case of beer, Timmy drove his all-terrain vehicle into a tree after swerving to avoid a rabbit. He wasn't wearing a helmet. We see Timmy rushed into the Shock Trauma Center with severe brain swelling as his parents wait tearfully for him to show signs of cognizance. After a week, he's released into a rehab center, where he must learn to speak and walk again. Five months later, as Timmy celebrates his 16th birthday, he's irritable and depressed, and he's begun drinking again. He has recently dropped out of high school and has spent a week in a mandatory detox program.

• **Andy, age 19:** Andy was driving home from a friend's house after "a few beers" when his Jeep, going 70 miles (112.7 km) per hour in a 35-mph (56.3 kph) zone, hit an embankment and rolled over four times. Lucky to be alive, Andy is brought into the Shock Trauma Center, where he admits to drinking six to nine beers every day. However, he claims that he's not an alcoholic and that he can control himself. Lying on the emergency room table, his head being stitched together, he agrees to "cut back" on his drinking.

• **Traci, age 18:** After "partying" one night, Traci got into a car with a drunk driver, who ended up speeding and slamming into a tree. Traci's head

Even if no one dies in a drunk-driving crash, the injuries caused can leave lifelong issues and problems. Brain injuries in particular can cause memory problems and even more serious issues.

Not only would a DUI conviction cost you and your family a lot of money in legal fees and potential fines, hospital bills for serious injuries can be extreme in the United States. It can take a long time for finances to recover, if they ever do.

smashed into the windshield, and her brain banged back and forth and twisted inside her skull. She was in a coma for 81 days. She also sustained multiple injuries so severe (a ruptured spleen, punctured lung, broken ribs, and smashed pelvis) that she was unable to do anything for herself. Her mother describes her as being "like an infant." Four years later, after painstaking rehabilitation, Traci still struggles with speaking (due to partial paralysis) and spends most of her time at home. About that fateful day, she says, "I just basically ruined my life."

• **Tom, age 17:** After drinking a quart of vodka at a local mall, Tom fell 20 feet (6.1 m) off a landing and onto a stone floor. Though he denies he's been drinking as he's brought into the Shock Trauma Center, tests confirm that he had consumed alcohol. His family arrives to find him drugged and breathing on a respirator. They wait and pray as doctors remove a dangerous blood clot in his frontal lobe. When Tom's friends come to visit, his mom implores them to change their ways. Since his accident, Tom has been unable to find a job.

• **Katie, age 16:** After meeting some guys she didn't know (and not realizing that they had been drinking), Katie recalls, "I thought the guy driving was pretty hot, so of course I got in the car with them." She ended up in a crash that left her in a coma for more than seven weeks. She also had a broken arm, a broken leg, and multiple internal injuries. Her mother describes the ensuing struggle to help Katie relearn basic functions, as well as enduring an angry phase (typical of head trauma victims) of lashing out, biting, and hitting. Katie's short-term memory is so impaired that she cannot learn properly or even enjoy a movie. She's given up her college plans and is looking for clerical work.

• **Warren, age 17:** One day, Warren got a lift home from a friend who had been drinking "a couple" of beers. When the friend's car crashed, Warren's brain, like Traci's, slammed back and forth inside his skull. He now has difficulty sleeping, eating, concentrating, and reading. Warren describes himself as having been "happy-go-lucky" before the crash, but he has since been hospitalized for severe depression. He's also developed aggression issues and has recently faced criminal charges. Warren is currently under house arrest for six months.

THE EMOTIONAL IMPACT

If you were lucky enough to survive a drunk-driving crash, you might feel happy or relieved. Or your feelings could be much more complicated than that. You may feel guilty if a loved one was hurt and you were not. You may feel anger toward the drunk driver who caused the crash. Maybe you were in the car with the drunk driver, and they are your relative or friend. It can be hard to forgive someone when they put your life at risk.

Whether you're the drunk driver, a victim, or a loved one of a victim, it's important to get help dealing with your feelings. Professionals such as school counselors, social workers, and therapists

After you or a loved one is in a drunk-driving accident, you may have a lot of emotions to process, including grief, anger, and guilt. Talking it out in a support group with others who understand can help.

are trained to help people work through powerful emotions like grief, guilt, and anger. Or, you might feel more comfortable turning to a favorite teacher, coach, or religious leader. Talking about your feelings will be difficult, but it may help. Try not to shut out family and friends. It may seem as if nobody understands what you're going through, but people do want to help.

If you're having trouble dealing with your feelings after a bad accident, it can help to talk to someone. Ask a trusted adult for help.

If someone you love was killed in a drunk-driving crash, you may experience many painful emotions. You probably feel intense sadness because that person is gone and intense anger toward the drunk driver. If it was your loved one who was driving drunk, you might feel angry with him or her. You might be ashamed that your loved one caused others to be hurt. If you knew that your loved one was too drunk to drive, you probably feel guilty about that too. You might even feel guilty that you're still alive. If you were drinking and driving and caused an accident, you are sure to feel many of these emotions as well.

Perhaps your loved one didn't die but is permanently disabled after a drunk-driving crash. This is also a very emotionally stressful situation. You're happy the person is alive, but it's difficult to see them disabled. You might even feel resentful that you now have to do many things that your loved one cannot do for themselves.

Support groups, whether in-person or online, provide a place for you to talk to others who have experienced similar tragedies. There are support groups for people who have lost a loved one. There are also support groups for people who are related to alcoholics or have been affected by alcohol.

WHEN IT'S TIME FOR HELP

A drunk-driving incident can be a big sign that a teen or adult has a serious problem with alcohol. They may be an alcoholic. If you or someone you know thinks about drinking alcohol all the time and can't stop drinking even if they want to, then it's time for professional help. This means the person needs to see a therapist with experience in substance abuse. They could also check out a support program such as Alcoholics Anonymous, where they can meet other people who may also need help.

Alcohol rehabilitation programs are designed to help people get over their dependence on alcohol. The person admitted will go through detox, which means they will stop drinking alcohol entirely. All the alcohol will leave their body. Sometimes this can cause symptoms of nausea, sweating, and headaches. Doctors at the rehab facility can help with these symptoms.

Another important part of rehab is counseling. Patients can talk with counselors and other patients in a support group setting about their problems, including why they drink and why they want to stop. They can also work on learning skills to say no when a drink is offered and how to take care of themselves better.

Going to a rehabilitation center can feel like a scary step, but sometimes it's the best way forward when it feels impossible to stop drinking alcohol.

DO SOMETHING

Sometimes, grief can spur positive action. Mothers Against Drunk Driving (MADD) is one example. Candy Lightner founded MADD in 1980 after her

If drinking starts to control a person's life, but they cannot stop using alcohol, it may be time for rehab. This is a place to go to learn how to live life without alcohol.

The first step against fighting drunk driving is never to do it. Beyond that, there are other ways to fight to make the roads safer for everyone.

daughter Cari was killed by a drunk driver. She turned her grief into positive steps by pursuing stricter laws and punishments for drunk drivers. Soon after the founding of MADD, Cari's friends organized SADD (Students Against Destructive Decisions; formerly Students Against Drunk Driving). That marked part of the beginning of teenagers' involvement in the fight against the fatal combination of alcohol and driving.

NOYS is a collaborative network of national organizations, federal agencies, and business and industry members, working together to promote youth safety and health. Both MADD and SADD are members, along with nearly 40 other organizations that focus on youth health and safety. YOUTH-Turn, an online tool sponsored by NOYS, is a resource that helps teens and community members turn adversity into educational and constructive opportunities. The goal is to prevent similar tragedies from happening to others.

You can get involved too, to help stop drunk driving. All you have to do is take the first step.

CHAPTER 6

MAKE A CHANGE

Today, teens are advocates for many causes that are important to them, such as efforts to combat climate change or for increasing school safety. If drinking and driving is an important issue that you would like to help with, you can! Teens today can change the world.

JOIN IN

If you'd like to help stop the problem of drinking and driving, one way to help is to look to already established organizations. By working with an already established organization, you can use its tools and resources to begin making a difference. Some teens feel that they have no power and that they could never change anything. But the truth is, you can.

These students are protesting drunk driving. You can organize a protest in your community too. Help get the word out and you could save lives.

STUDENTS AGAINST DRUNK DRIVING

Check out a student group, such as SADD. When it was created, the purpose of Students Against Drunk Driving was to do just that: stop drinking and driving. But now the group has a wider focus, helping

SADD, MADD, and other groups sometimes have events to educate students about drunk driving. Perhaps you could organize one at your school!

improve the health and safety of teens through peer-to-peer education. SADD works on issues such as traffic safety but also substance abuse and physical and emotional health. The group works to prevent teen suicide, anxiety, and depression as well.

MOTHERS AGAINST DRUNK DRIVING

MADD, Mothers Against Drunk Driving, has done a great deal of work to change drunk-driving laws in the United States. It has succeeded in achieving major legislative changes, including:

- Passage of the National Minimum Drinking Age Act
- Stiffer fines and jail sentences for driving while intoxicated
- Lobbying for a national 0.08 BAC per se law
- Lobbying for a federal zero tolerance law

You can help MADD with its mission in many different ways. There are advocacy efforts, in which you can support changes happening in Congress. You can work to help raise awareness in your community. And you can come up with your own ideas too.

If you'd like to get involved with SADD, or learn more about what it does, check out its website, www.sadd.org. You can see if your high school has a SADD chapter. If not, gather a group of interested and dedicated classmates. Contact the SADD national office to register your chapter.

BE CREATIVE

Teens today are often a lot savvier than most adults when it comes to social media. You can use that know-how to start your own anti-drunk driving initiative. Make sure to get organized before you pitch your ideas to your school superintendent and principal. Presenting a responsible, organized plan is more likely to earn you respect and the green light to go ahead with your project.

GET SOCIAL

Good social media skills are in demand. Create a social media campaign or develop a hashtag about not drinking, buckling up, and staying alive. Get a viral campaign going. Work with your friends to come up with a catchy slogan or to create attention-grabbing images.

You don't always have to start from scratch either. If you cannot think of a campaign, use existing campaigns from SADD ("21 or Bust" or "Think About It . . . Is It Worth the Risk?") and NHTSA ("You Drink, You Drive, You Lose" or "Over the Limit, Under Arrest"). Using national campaigns usually

Working together, you and your friends could come up with a great campaign to fight drunk driving in your community.

Prom can be a night that you'll always remember. Make sure it's a great memory by planning your rides ahead of time. Whether in a limo, a car, or a parent's minivan, you can have fun with your friends.

A DIFFERENT KIND OF PROMPOSAL

Prom night can be a really fun evening for you and your friends to dress up and cut loose. It can also be a deadly night if you're not careful. About 1,000 people under the age of 21 die each year in preventable accidents during prom and graduation celebrations, according to the National Highway Traffic Safety Administration.

So, before you head out on prom night, be sure to plan ahead. The best choice is to simply avoid drinking alcohol. Select a designated sober driver if you've made the decision to drink or think there's even a chance you might be around alcohol.

You can even consider having a parent chauffeur, using a ride share service, or saving up for a limo if that's in your budget. Some teens even opt to host a late-night party at their school or at their homes, so they can all have a great—and safe—time together. There are so many ways to have fun, just be creative and plan ahead!

allows you to access online resources. You can check out their websites to be sure.

You can even organize an online or in-person event that could attract media coverage. Work with your friends to plan a rally or an event with a panel of speakers. Panelists to consider include drunk-driving victims, teens, emergency room nurses or physicians, other health professionals or experts, law enforcement officials, and parents. Plan for a car crash demonstration. Be sure that adults are involved, but make it a teen-led initiative. Your campaign will have more power if it comes from you.

REMEMBER THE YOUNGER KIDS

Who did you look up to when you were younger? Kids a few years older than you, probably. Remember how cool you thought high school students were when you were in middle school? Think of the influence you could have if you reached out to kids a few years behind you in school. If you were to share with them the dangers of drunk driving, you could have a real impact.

What about running a poster or slogan contests in the elementary and junior high schools in your town? Interact with younger students and teach them what you know about the dangers of drugs and alcohol. Solicit local businesses and law enforcement agencies to donate prizes (such as free pizza or movie tickets) to entice younger kids to make a commitment to stay away from alcohol.

ACT SAFELY

The most important act you can do regarding drinking and driving is to never get in a car with someone who's been drinking and to never drive after you've had a drink. Preparing before you go out can help make sure you stay safe.

It's important to be a good example to younger students. In fact, that may be one of the most important things you can do to help fight drunk driving in the future!

VOLUNTEER TO BE THE SOBER DRIVER

If you drink or hang out with people who do, protect yourself by using the designated driver system. A designated driver is someone who volunteers to drive on an occasion when others will be drinking.

A designated driver shouldn't drink alcohol at all while they're the DD, not even a sip. That's the only way to be positive they're safe.

In Sweden and England, where this idea started, designated drivers put their car keys in their empty glass so that no one would serve them alcohol.

Having a designated driver ensures that everyone will have a safe ride home. At the next party, someone else from the group takes their turn being

the designated driver. The driver must be someone you can trust so that when the designated driver says they haven't had anything to drink, you know it's the truth.

People who say, "Well, I haven't had *that* much to drink, I can still drive," are a dangerous choice for designated driver. The social drinker, as well as the alcoholic, can still be a menace on the road. Social drinkers can be impaired because their judgment, reaction time, and coordination are affected. Remember how easily just one drink can affect your vision, reaction time, and reflexes. The safest way to get home from a party is with a completely sober driver.

SIGN ON THE DOTTED LINE

A pact is an agreement that both teens and parents can live with and will follow through on if the need arises. A teen and their parents sign a formal, written agreement that acknowledges the potential problems in drinking and driving. It also states that you both agree to do something about it. For example, a teen can agree to call a parent to pick them up any time they face a risky situation. With a teen/parent pact, teens can face a potentially dangerous situation with confidence, knowing they have parental support in dealing with it. This can alleviate the pressure to get into a car with a drunk driver. The contract must also address situations in which the teen is the one who's had too much to drink and is driving and responsible for others.

The other side of the coin is a clause in the contract in which the parents agree to the same conditions—that the mother or father won't drink and drive or be a passenger in a car with a drunk driver. SADD has created a pact called the "Contract for Life" that a teenager can sign along with his or her parents.

Especially when you're new to driving, it's very important to be careful about both everyday rules and challenges (such as checking behind you when backing up) and more specific ones (such as saying no to alcohol and drunk driving).

The young person's agreement and the parent's agreement look like this:

YOUNG PERSON'S AGREEMENT:

I recognize that there are many potentially destructive decisions I face every day and commit to you that I will do everything in my power to avoid making decisions that will jeopardize my health, my safety and overall well-being, or your trust in me. I understand the dangers associated with the use of alcohol and drugs and the destructive behaviors often associated with impairment.

By signing below, I pledge my best effort to remain free from alcohol and drugs; I agree that I will never drive under the influence; I agree that I will never ride with an impaired driver; and I agree that I will always wear a seat belt.

Finally, I agree to call you if I am ever in a situation that threatens my safety and to communicate with you regularly about issues of importance to both of us.

CARING ADULT'S AGREEMENT:

I am committed to you and to your health and safety. By signing below, I pledge to do everything in my power to understand and communicate with you about the many difficult and potentially destructive decisions you face.

Further, I agree to provide for your safe, sober transportation home if you are ever in a situation that threatens your safety and to defer discussions about that situation until a time when we can both talk about it in a calm and caring manner.

I also pledge to you that I will not drive under the influence of alcohol or drugs, I will always seek safe, sober transportation home, and I will always wear a seat belt.

Communication is important. Pacts like the ones shown here help make sure that both adults and teens are on the same page.

Working out a contract enables teens and parents to open the door to deeper trust and communication. It also lets teens see that parents can have similar problems. Equal responsibilities, with no double standards, are the goals of a successful teen/parent pact.

Contracts and pacts can allow teens to talk about their fears and what's really going on in their lives. They can also keep a cloak of parental protection around teens at a time when they often resist parental interference. In addition, they give parents a chance to talk about their own concerns and show their love.

But you must really mean it. There must be a sincere effort on both sides to maintain the agreement. The contract is your agreement to act responsibly so that your parents can have more trust in you. That's the goal. The more trust you earn, the more freedom you'll get. Isn't that worth it?

SAFE RIDES

Safe ride programs offer rides home to teens who don't want to ride with someone who's been drinking. Many local organizations, cities, and college campuses have instituted this kind of program.

There's a lot of preparation for safe rides, and some liability is involved, so you'll need help and supervision to create a program. Enlisting the aid of a local service organization may get you off to a good start.

Showing your parents that you're a safe and responsible driver might put you on the road to more freedom!

Some communities plan to provide rides from 10 p.m. to 3 a.m. on Friday and Saturday nights. Using cell phones and even walkie-talkies, parents and other adults in the community can get involved. It's a good idea for adults to drive in teams of two or three. Drivers should keep records of picked-up teens, times, and addresses. It's important to set up guidelines for confidentiality and to use seat belts and safe cars.

For a more informal plan, several families can set up pacts to provide "parent taxis." Maybe your best friend's father is willing to be on duty this weekend for your friends in case a safe ride is needed after a party or a concert. Next weekend could be your

By planning ahead and staying sober, you can have fun out on the road with your friends. Just think for yourself, follow the rules, and stay safe!

mother's or older brother's turn. Most families are glad to work out this kind of arrangement if you ask and set up some guidelines beforehand.

Ride-share apps can also be a help when you need a lift home, though most companics have rules that say their passengers need to be 18 years old. You'll also need a credit card to create an account. Talk it over with your parents and see what works best for you and your family

BE SMART!

Drunk driving is a serious problem. About one person dies every 48 minutes from a drunk-driving accident, according to the National Highway Traffic Safety Administration. But that doesn't mean you can't make a difference. You can plan ahead so you never drink and drive. You can help your friends by informing them of the seriousness of the problem. You can be the sober driver. You can make a difference in the number of people whose lives are changed by drunk driving each year. Smart teens can change the world!

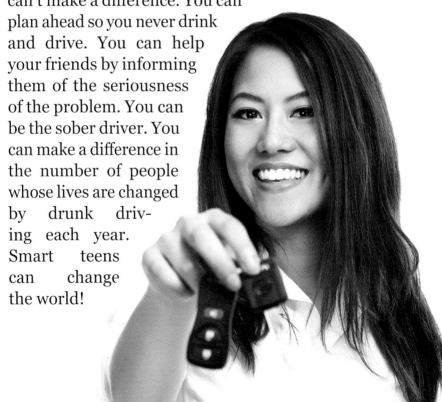

GLOSSARY

advocacy: Public support for a policy change, usually for a particular cause.

alcohol dependence: A pattern of alcohol use in which the person shows tolerance, withdrawal symptoms, lack of control when drinking, preoccupation with alcohol, and use of alcohol despite physical and psychological consequences.

alcoholic: A person who suffers from alcohol use disorder, a chronic disease where the person has an uncontrollable obsession with alcohol.

alcohol use disorder: A disease involving uncontrollable drinking and obsession with alcohol.

binge drinking: Drinking more than five alcoholic beverages (four for females) in a period of about two hours.

blood alcohol content (BAC): The concentration of alcohol in the blood, used as a measure of the degree of intoxication in an individual.

central nervous system: The part of the body that controls and coordinates all activity, consisting of the brain and spinal cord.

cognizance: Awareness.

coma: A state of deep, prolonged unconsciousness, generally caused by injury or disease. The person cannot be roused and does not respond to external stimuli.

depressant: An agent, especially a drug, which decreases the rate of vital activities in the body.

detox: A treatment designed to remove toxins from the body; short for "detoxify."

ignition interlock: A device hooked up to a car. A drunk driving offender may have to blow into the tube to test their BAC before the car will start.

GLOSSARY 97

impaired: Functioning poorly or inadequately; intoxicated by alcohol or drugs.

intoxicated: Affected by alcohol or drugs; drunk. Showing diminished mental and physical capabilities.

negligence: Failure to exercise the degree of care that the law requires for the protection of other people.

passenger: Anyone in a motor vehicle who is not the driver.

peer pressure: Social pressure from friends or a peer group that is intended to convince someone to change their behavior in order to fit in.

prefrontal cortex: Located in the front of the brain, the section responsible for planning and impulse control.

revocation: The act of withdrawing or canceling.

sober: Not intoxicated or drunk; not under the influence of alcohol or drugs.

sobriety checkpoint: A roadblock where law enforcement officials stop all vehicles to investigate the possibility of impaired driving.

tolerance: A condition in which higher doses of a drug are required to produce the same effect as experienced initially.

treatment: Activities designed to change a pattern of unhealthy behavior, such as that which occurs with alcohol dependence or addiction. Activities can include detoxification, counseling, and education.

zero tolerance: The policy of applying penalties to even minor infringements of a law in order to reinforce its importance.

FOR MORE INFORMATION

ASPIRA National Office
1220 L Street NW, Suite 701
Washington, DC 20005
(202) 835-3600
Website: www.aspira.org
Twitter: @ASPIRA_national
Facebook: @ASPIRA.ASSOCIATION
Instagram: @ aspira_assoc
A nonprofit dedicated to developing the education
of the Latino community, including traffic safety
issues such as seat belt use and alcohol awareness.

Mothers Against Drunk Driving (MADD)
511 East John Carpenter Freeway
Irving, TX 75062
(800) ASK-MADD [275-6233]
Website: www.madd.org
Twitter: @MADDOnline
Facebook: @MADD.Official
Instagram: @mothersagainstdrunkdriving
Since 1980, MADD has been fighting to stop
drunk driving, support the victims of this violent
crime, and prevent underage drinking. The organization has worked toward comprehensive legislative changes, social campaigns, and much more.

**National Highway Traffic Safety Adminis-
tration (NHTSA)**
1200 New Jersey Avenue, SE

Washington, DC 20590
(888) 327-4236
Website: ww.nhtsa.gov
Facebook: @NHTSA
Instagram: @nhtsagov
Twitter: @nhtsagov
This U.S. government agency has a great deal
of resources, research, and statistics on driving
and safety. Campaigns to curtail drunk driving
include, "Drive Sober or Get Pulled Over."

National Organizations for Youth Safety (NOYS)

950 N. Washington Street
Suite 317
Alexandia, VA 22314
(571) 368-4090
Website: www.noys.org
Facebook: @NationalOrganizationsforYouth-
Safety
Instagram: @noysnews/
Twitter: @NOYSnews
NOYS is a coalition of organizations, federal agen-
cies, and business and industry members that all
strive to serve young people. The group provides
useful resources on underage drinking and driv-
ing, substance abuse, and many other issues.

SADD Alberta

P.O. Box 7220
Calgary, AB T2P 3M1

Canada
(403) 313-SADD (7233)
Website: www.saddalberta.com
E-mail: info@saddalberta.com
SADD Alberta works to stop drinking and driving in Canada. SADD Alberta empowers teens through virtual speaker series, campaigns, and contests.

Substance Abuse and Mental Health Services Administration
5600 Fishers Lane
Rockville, MD 20857
(877) SAMHSA-7 (726-4727)
Website: www.samhsa.gov
Facebook: @samhsa
Twitter: @samhsagov
This U.S. government agency is dedicated to reducing substance abuse and mental illness. A national helpline, treatment opportunities, and research work to help those dependent on drugs and alcohol.

Transport Canada
330 Sparks Street
Ottawa, ON K1A 0N5
Canada
(866) 995-9737
Website: www.tc.gc.ca
Email: questions@tc.gc.ca

Facebook: @TransportandInfrastructureinCanada
Instagram: @TransportCanada
Twitter: @transport_gc
Transport Canada is a department within the government of Canada. It works to provide efficient and safe transportation systems throughout the country.

FOR FURTHER READING

Glasgow, Kathleen. *You'd Be Home* Now. New York, NY: Delcorte Press, 2021.

Gordon, Sherri M. *Teens and Addiction.* New York, NY: Rosen Publishing, 2019.

Hurt, Avery E. *Alcohol.* New York, NY: Rosen Publishing, 2019.

Kamal, Sheena. *Fight Like a Girl.* New York, NY: Penguin Teen, 2021.

Krumsiek, Allison. *Teens and Alcohol: A Dangerous Combination.* New York, NY: Lucent, 2019.

Landau, Jennifer. *Teens Talk About Drugs and Alcohol.* New York, NY: Rosen Publishing, 2018.

Mason, Lizzy. *The Art of Losing.* New York, NY: Soho Teen, 2019.

Peters, Jennifer. *Alcohol Abuse.* New York, NY: Rosen Publishing, 2019.

Simms, Jennifer. *Teens and Distracting Driving.* San Diego, CA: ReferencePoint Press, Inc., 2019.

INDEX

ABOUT THE AUTHOR

Elissa Bongiorno is a journalist who has been published in *USA Weekend*, the *Baltimore Sun*, and *In Touch Weekly*, among other publications. She received her master's in journalism from the University of Maryland and has written more than a dozen other titles for students, including *Coping with Stress*, *Coping with HIV/AIDS*, and *James Till and Ernest McCulloch: The Team That Discovered Stem Cells*.

CREDITS